CONTENTS

INTRODUCTION

Do you ever feel that we need a lot of *stuff* in order to worship in the modern church?

Before we even begin to engage with God we often have to set up the PA system, rehearse the band, prepare the visual projection and round up the trained ministry team. Or perhaps in other traditions you might need to find an ordained priest, prepare a choir and gather all the right cups, robes and furniture. Another kind of church might assemble the creative worship team, choreograph a dance, arrange the lights and smoke machines, and plan a response which requires 300 candles, stones and post-it notes...

All of these things can be very helpful. In fact, God in his grace loves to make use of our songs, technology, traditions, leadership, creativity and more. He transforms them into things which point to him and enrich our times together. He blesses all kinds of styles, and loves to use our gifts and efforts in drawing people into his presence.

The problem is that we can start to think that these outer "things", these communication methods and human traditions, are fundamental and essential for worship. The liberating truth is that they are not!

Back to the heart

Think of a wedding day. Some couples get very hung up on whether the dress is right, the cake is perfect, or if the reception band plays the right songs. But all of this is just "outer stuff", which ought to be serving the true heart of the day. The important questions are: do the couple love one another? Did they commit to a lifetime together? Did the guests support them and

celebrate their relationship? Everything else should serve and point towards these goals.

In a similar way, simple worship reminds us that *God* is the centre of our worship. It reminds us that worship is only possible because we come to the Father through Jesus Christ, in the power of the Holy Spirit. When all the other bits and bobs are swept aside, we begin to see the very heart of worship: Jesus' death and resurrection has made the way for us to enter into God's presence. As Paul puts it in one of his letters:

> "Now all of us can come to the Father through the same Holy Spirit because of what Christ has done for us." Eph. 2:18, (NLT).

This means that all the other things we worry about might not be vital as we thought. Did you play that song badly? Did someone choose the wrong prayer? Was the projector not working properly? Did the candles blow out? Don't panic! These

were not the things that made your worship "work"; they were not the point of it all. God makes worship "work". God is the point of it all.

When all is stripped away

Sometimes, in order to remind ourselves that it is not all about us or our efforts, it is helpful to choose to strip some of the "outer stuff" away from our worship. Soul Survivor church in Watford did something like this. It was a period where on the outside everything seemed to be going really well - they had Matt Redman and other great worship leaders. They had full bands with guitars and drums and keyboards. They had new songs, projection screens and enthusiastic congregations. However, not everything was as it seemed. Matt Redman writes:

known song "When the Music Fades". When other things are stripped away, we can be reminded that our worship is all about Jesus.

> "We realised some of the things we thought were helping us in our worship were actually hindering us. They were throwing us off the scent of what it really means to worship... somehow we'd started to rely on these things a little too much, and they'd become distractions... Mike [Pilavachi] decided on a pretty drastic course of action: we'd strip everything away for a season, just to see where our hearts were."
>
> Matt Redman, The Unquenchable Worshipper, pages 76-77.

Some potential pitfalls

Perhaps one danger with a book like this is that people could think we are advocating "lazy worship", "half-hearted worship" or "poorly-planned worship". This is not our intention - God deserves nothing less than our full devotion. Good preparation honours him and our congregations. Our worship should be a "sacrifice of praise". However, notice that when the book of Hebrews uses that phrase, the writer begins:

> "Through Jesus, therefore, let us continually offer to God a sacrifice of praise"   Heb. 13:15.

Soul Survivor "banned the band" for a few months in 1997. They admit that to begin with it was unpopular and awkward. But ultimately it helped them to take their focus off the things which were good, but not ultimately what worship is about. It led to a much richer understanding of worship, and as a result Matt Redman wrote the well-

We come and bring our sacrifice of worship *through Jesus*. Our best efforts honour God only because Christ makes them worthy. Give your all, but never stop trusting in God.

Another potential pitfall related to this book is that "simple" can sound like simplistic, naive, or immature. One of our friends recently shared this sentiment on social

media: "Simplicity is highly overrated. Down with the prejudice against complexity!" We know what he means. Being a Christian in contemporary society is complex. Simple worship is not about easy answers. It is not about "dumbing down", rejecting 2000 years of church history, or trying to pretend that your congregation is not made up of a very diverse set of people, each with their own struggles.

It is also not about putting a "vintage" sepia filter on our worship: hiding the technology and bringing out the banjos and candles in order to fake a version of authenticity. Simplicity in worship does not look any one particular way. Nor does any one "method" guarantee a heartfelt connection with God.

What we are advocating is intentionally stepping away from things which are needlessly complicated or distracting, in order to focus on the one who is really important - God. This is actually quite radical, because "radical" comes from the word "roots" (in Latin). It is about getting back to the roots, the basics of what it really means to engage with God.

Look into your heart

Ultimately, this process needs to begin in each of our hearts. Jesus is primarily concerned that his friends spend time with him, as we see in the story of Mary and Martha. In what ways are you like Martha - running around trying to do things for Jesus? They might be good things: service, creativity, leadership, hospitality. But are you so "distracted by the preparations" (Luke 10:40) for worship that you may miss hearing Jesus' call to simply be with him?

> "You are worried and upset about many things, but few things are needed - or indeed only one."
> *Luke 10:41-42.*

Some questions for reflection/discussion:

What are you "worried or upset" about? What distracts you from coming to Jesus simply?

Mary made the "one thing" - being with Jesus - her priority. What would that look like for you?

How could you submit all other activities, efforts and expressions to the service of that one goal?

SIMPLE SMALL-GROUP WORSHIP

Some people choose simple worship, others have simplicity thrust upon them. This is often the case in a small group - whether that means a Bible study, prayer triplet, missional community, youth group, or another setting. In these contexts you do not have the big band, church organ, ordained minister or drama team to help you worship. In many cases, small groups will conclude "we can't worship together - we don't have the resources."

What a tragedy! Jesus has made the way for you to worship God by the Holy Spirit. You don't technically need anything else. The way is open. And by his grace God has also given you other gifts to help you engage with him. He has given you the Bible and his creation all around you. He has given you the gifts of your group: storytelling, art, cooking, the setting up of a room, instrumental music, and more. He has given you 2000 years of Christian prayers, postures and spiritual practices to draw from. He has given you silence. Let's not think "we can't worship in our small group". You have more than you need.

Less than perfect situations

All over the world, people worship God in less than perfect scenarios. The heritage of Paul and Silas singing songs of worship in prison (Acts 16:25) is played out across the globe. Right now, secret house churches meet covertly in countries of persecution, whispering hymns and prayers. Churches without Bibles recite precious scripture passages from memory. Communities hit by natural disasters sing songs of hope,

with no accompaniment but their dogged faith in the God who is bigger than their circumstances.

We in the West need to learn from the "simple" worship of our brothers and sisters who lack all the bells and whistles we drag into worship. Our small groups can be places of genuine devotion and engagement with God, making the most of whatever gifts and resources he has given us in our context.

Make the most of your size

Sometimes worship in a large church can feel impersonal because there is not the space for interaction and conversation. In a small group you can take advantage of your smaller size by encouraging people to talk. Invite people to share reasons why they praise or thank God this week, or ask them to mention problems or struggles for intercessory prayer. Some of the worship ideas that follow give suggestions for ways to do this that are creative and non-threatening.

Take your time

Sunday services are often packed with things which *have* to be included. There can also be a concern to keep things moving, to maintain the interest of those with short attention spans. Another benefit of the small-group is that you can take your time, slow down and stretch things out.

For example: rather than reading scripture quickly and then moving on, why not read it one sentence at a time, pausing for 30 seconds between each section to reflect? Instead of singing three songs, why not sing one and leave instrumental sections in between the verses? If someone shares a need, take a pause in the middle of your meeting to pray for them.

Use the gifts

As much contemporary worship becomes more "professionalised" and takes on the tone of a show presented from the stage, smaller group worship can encourage another dynamic. You can celebrate the "folk creativity" of your group, making use of the variety of gifts. Do you have poets, artists, bakers, photographers, animators, flower arrangers... and more? All of these gifts can be included in your worship if you allow them space. Small groups can also be a place to experiment with new ideas, and develop leaders who are not yet confident enough to get up in front of a whole church congregation.

We hope the ideas in this chapter will get you started, but don't be limited just to what follows - almost all of the resources in this book are adaptable for small group use.

Some questions for reflection/discussion:

What is your experience of worshipping in a small group? What has worked and what has been difficult?

What gifts do people in your small group have? How could you encourage people to use these in leading worship?

Read the passage about Paul and Silas in jail (Acts 16:22-34). Have you heard any stories about worship in the persecuted church? What do you find inspirational about these stories?

P S A L M S

The book of Psalms is a rich and under-used resource for contemporary worship. In the past, the church has sung them to chant melodies (which avoids the problem of irregular line-length), or re-written them to have equal syllables (such as John Calvin's metrical psalms; see **genevanpsalter.com**). You might explore some of those ideas, or try our suggestions on the following pages to engage with "the Church's song-book" in your small-group's times of worship.

Psalms Praise

This is an idea we use and share often. It is very simple, but encourages biblically-rooted, participative and inspiring worship. All you need is for each person to have a Bible in their hands.

Encourage the group to open up the book of Psalms. We often sing a simple chorus to start, and then invite the group to read one line or one verse from a psalm that strikes them. It could be a favourite verse, one that is particularly relevant, or just something which catches their eye. The group can respond with an "Amen" or another encouragement, and then someone else can read. You can keep a chord or a rhythm going underneath if someone is playing an instrument, and you can sing your chorus again to finish if you like, but his works just as well without music.

Reading with different frames

The most basic way to engage with a psalm is to read one together. Distribute Bibles or a print-out of the words, and then speak the psalm out together. You may wish to pause after each verse, or stop and give space for prayers that are inspired by phrases from the psalm.

A way to develop this further is to view a psalm through different historical "frames". This will involve some preparation for the leader, but it can be very fruitful. For example, you could introduce a psalm using one or a number of the following:

- **Old Testament frame**: Does this psalm come out of the life of a character like David (23, 51) or Solomon (72)? Does it relate to the temple (30), or the exile (137)? Could you read a related passage of scripture, or paint a picture of its original context? As with all of these "frames", the point is not so much to have a deep Bible study on the psalm, but to experience it worshipfully from a fresh perspective.

- **Jesus frame**: some psalms point towards the Messiah (24, 72, 110), whilst others were quoted by Jesus (22). Jesus would have sung all of the psalms as he grew up, including on the night he was betrayed (probably a passover hymn, 113-118, see Matt. 26-30). What does it mean to see this psalm through the eyes of Jesus? This may also help as you wrestle with some of the more difficult and violent psalms.

- **Body of Christ frame**: We may struggle to relate to a particular psalm ourselves, but it can make more sense when we see it through the eyes of a brother or sister. Across history and throughout the world people struggle and suffer. What does it mean to read a psalm through the eyes of someone suffering a natural disaster, or religious persecution, or war, or homelessness? Could you use images, newspapers or reports from persecuted churches to bring this to life for your group? Reflect on these worshipfully, turning to God in prayer, lament and honest cries from the heart.

(This idea came from a talk by John Witvliet at London School of Theology, February 24, 2015.)

Emotions in the Psalms

When we are going through difficult times it can sometimes be hard to be honest with God about how we feel. There are situations in our lives, or when we see an injustice or a tragedy happening in the world, when we struggle to find ways to pray. The Psalms give us language to be entirely open with God. As we are honest with him, this can be a door to receiving his perspective on the situation, his empowering to make a difference, and even his healing for deep wounds.

> "[In the Psalms] the prayer life of the speaker is filled with anger and rawness. There is no attempt to be polite or docile. Psalmic prayer practises no cover-up. Real prayer is being open about the negatives and yielding them to God... they are never yielded unless they be fully expressed."
>
> Walter Brueggemann, *The Message of the Psalms*, page 66.

Classical music

One of our friends, Ron Jones, has developed a way of using the Psalms which helps to tap into these emotions. He chooses some of the more difficult, lamenting psalms, and then finds appropriate classical music to fit the mood (you could try this, or use another style of music which better fits your group).

He plays the music from a CD and encourages the group to read the psalm aloud with whatever emotion is expressed in the text, whether that be doubt, fear, anger or another feeling. The individuals can reflect on whether these words apply to their own situation, or if they could be speaking and praying them on behalf of someone else - a friend, or someone they have seen on the news. In this way we can either express the ways we relate to the emotion of the psalm, or stand in solidarity with other people who do.

Ron's suggested music

Psalm 8:
Jehan Alain, "Choral Dorien".

Psalm 10:
Vaughn Williams, "Symphony no. 6", 1st movement.

Psalm 42:
Herbert Howells, "Like as the hart".

Psalm 42, 43:
Sibelius, "Symphony no. 6", 4th movement (opening).

Psalm 94:
Reubke, "Sonata on Psalm 94".

Other appropriate pieces:

Prokofiev: "Symphony No. 7", 1st movement.

Tchaikovsky: "Symphony No. 5," 2nd movement (first 4 minutes).

Herbert Howells: "Paean".

Langlais: "Incantation pour un jour saint".

JS Bach: "Cello Suite No. 5", sarabande.

Your own words

Another way of approaching emotions in the Psalms is to invite everyone in the group to re-write the text in their own words. They could use the kind of language and images that come naturally to them. They can also relate the emotions of the psalm to their own experiences, or situations in the world they are praying for. This opens up a creative space for people to relate the words of the psalmist to their contemporary experience.

Singing a refrain

If you want to start using music with the Psalms, using a refrain can be a good place to begin. Often, part of the psalm will be repeated, similar to a chorus in a modern song. Alternatively, you might be able to choose one verse or phrase which you feel is appropriate to sing, or use a chorus from an existing song. You can then read the rest of the verses, and insert the refrain at relevant points.

We have done this with Psalm 67, by singing the refrain (verse 3) to a slightly adapted version of the first line of the hymn "Holy, Holy, Holy". Alternatively, you could make up your own tune. We have then inserted moments for silent or open prayer, inspired by the words of the psalm.

Feel free to copy the page opposite and hand it out to your group. Alternatively, if you have a computer screen you could download the PowerPoint from this web page, which includes engaging imagery behind the words:

engageworship.org/Psalm67

May the peo-ples praise you, God; may all the peo-ples praise you.

Tune Public Domain

Further refrain ideas:

- Read out Psalm 23, and sing Stuart Townend's chorus from "The Lord's My Shepherd" as a refrain.

- Read out Psalm 103, and use Matt Redman and Jonas Myrin's "Bless the Lord (10,000 Reasons)" chorus as a refrain.

- Read out Psalm 136, and after each line sing the Chris Tomlin tune to "His love endures forever" from "Give Thanks to the Lord". You could then also speak out your own personal lines of thankfulness to God, responding each time with the refrain.

- Read out Psalm 145, and use the first two lines of Graham Ord's "The Lord is Gracious and Compassionate" as a refrain.

Psalm 67 Worship Flow

SING: May the peoples praise you, God;
    may all the peoples praise you.

SAY: May God be gracious to us and bless us
    and make his face shine on us –

[Pause for silent or open prayers for needs in your church community.]

———————

SING: May the peoples praise you, God;
    may all the peoples praise you.

SAY: so that your ways may be known on earth,
    your salvation among all nations.

[Pause for silent or open prayers for needs across the world.]

———————

SING: May the peoples praise you, God;
    may all the peoples praise you.

SAY: May the nations be glad and sing for joy,
    for you rule the peoples with equity
    and guide the nations of the earth.

[Pause for silent or open prayers for governments, elections and leaders.]

———————

SING: May the peoples praise you, God;
    may all the peoples praise you.

SAY: The land yields its harvest;
    God, our God, blesses us.

[Pause for silent or open prayers of thanks for God's provision.]

———————

SAY: May God bless us still,
    so that all the ends of the earth will fear him.

SING: May the peoples praise you, God;
    may all the peoples praise you.

CREATING

You might recognise a need for your small group members to express some of the things going on in their lives and hearts, things that are not always easy to articulate in words. The following ideas use visual and tactile creativity to help each person reflect on their life before God. We have often found that people will open up as they engage in these activities, sharing and praying more deeply than if we had just invited people to speak.

Collage

You will need:
Pile of magazines with attractive images, colours and headlines.
A3 paper.
Scissors and glue.

Encourage everyone to grab a magazine, and to tear out pictures or headlines which express an aspect of their relationship with God at that moment. We have found that even people who do not consider themselves "creative types" enjoy this process, and those who say they "can't draw" feel safe engaging with collage.

Each person can then arrange these on the A3 paper, and stick them down. Once

you are all finished you can invite people to talk about what they have created, as openly as they feel comfortable.

As a follow-up, you could pray for each other based on what was shared. It might also be interesting to bring these pictures back after a month or so, and invite people to share if anything has changed in the meantime. Or you could let everyone take someone else's picture home, and use it as a reminder to pray for them.

Play-dough

You can use play-dough (or home-made modelling clay) in all sorts of ways within worship. One of the simplest is to give everyone a piece, and ask them to form a shape of how they feel before God right then. People will make all sorts of things - a splat, a smiley face, a broken pot - there are no limits. Keep the mood light and feel free to laugh if your creation does not go quite according to plan!

Then, as with the collage activity, invite everyone to share about what they have made. At the end of your time, an extension of the idea is to invite people to re-mould their clay. They could make a shape that represents how they want to be before God in the coming week.

We have also used this medium when thinking about the incarnation of Jesus, "God with us" (Matt. 1:23), the "Word made flesh" (John 1:14) (thanks to Andy Stinson for this idea). We have placed our clay models on a table, and then formed a "Jesus" figure out of the same material and in the same size. We have reflected that Jesus was made of the same human stuff as us, that he understands our weakness and stands alongside us in our struggles.

A third way of using play-dough or clay is to reflect on the story in Jeremiah 18:1-4. God remoulds and remakes Israel like a potter with the clay. Dave Hopwood has written a reflection on this, which you can download for free from:

engageworship.org/ThePotter

"So I went to the potter's house, and sure enough, the potter was there, working away at his wheel. Whenever the pot the potter was working on turned out badly, as sometimes happens when you are working with clay, the potter would simply start over and use the same clay to make another pot."

Jer. 18:3-4, (MSG).

EVERYDAY OBJECTS

Simple, everyday objects can be used as a basis for worship reflections. This is helpful within the worship time, as you can touch and interact with the object. It also extends out to the daily life of the group, as when they see such an object again they can be reminded of how God spoke to them through it. Using ordinary objects in worship can help your group begin to see the world around them through God's eyes.

Simple way to start

One easy idea is to put 5-10 objects on a table in the centre of the room (for example: a candlestick; a decorative sculpture; a towel; an apple and so on - whatever you can find). Invite the group to look at the objects for a few minutes, asking God to reveal something about himself through the different things. When the right amount of time has passed, ask anyone who wishes to, to share their thoughts. You will be amazed how this simple way of focussing our thoughts can help us open up our hearts to God.

Reflecting God's Glory

On the next page is a small group meditation, based on Colossians 2:10 and 2 Corinthians 3:18. Thanks to Angela Bryan for sharing this idea with us.

You will need:
A whiteboard marker.
A small mirror.

Encourage the group to make themselves comfortable. You might want to play some soft, instrumental background music. Speak the words of the text on the next page.

Reflecting God's Glory

"We are God's masterpiece. He has created us anew in Christ Jesus, so we can do the good things he planned for us long ago." (Col 2:10 NLT.) [Pause...]

"We are God's workmanship, created in Christ Jesus to do good works, which God prepared in advance for us to do." (Col 2:10 NIV.) [Pause...]

Crafted, created, by the divine creator - intricate, beautiful, mysterious bodies, souls, hearts and minds.
We are sculpted and fashioned into a masterpiece for the Almighty to hang upon the wall of heaven and declare before all the angels: "it is good!"
We are created and saved by the same hands, the hands that "threw stars into space, to cruel nails surrendered." The very same hands. [Pause...]

Do you find it easier to think of yourself as a sinner, or as a masterpiece of God's creation? [Pause...]

We are both, but because of Jesus it is the masterpiece that God sees when he looks at us. Receive his delight in you today. [Pause...]

What good works have you been up to, that God prepared for you in advance?
What good works might God be preparing for you this week, this month, this year? [Pause...]

The good news is for everyone, in every circumstance and difficulty.
What might the good news mean for those closest to you? [Pause...]

"We, who with unveiled faces all reflect the Lord's glory,
are being transformed into his likeness with ever-increasing glory,
which comes from the Lord, who is the Spirit." (2 Cor. 3:18 NIV.)

What veils your face, hiding the good news from others' view?
What area of your life do you long to see transformed into his likeness?
Offer that to God now. [Pause...]

We reflect God's character to those around us.
We reflect the good news we have received to people we know.
Whose life do you long to reflect good news into?

> [Pass the mirror and pen around the group, for people to write onto the mirror the name of someone they want to reflect the good news to. Extend the prayerful silence depending on the group's response...]

Father, we long to reflect your likeness and embody your good news.
Continue to transform us, we pray, by your Spirit.
Thank you, Jesus, for creating us and saving us with the same hands,
and for giving us good works to do as we freely respond to your grace.
Father, Son, Spirit, live in us and work through us. Amen.

GARDEN WORSHIP

God speaks to us through his creation, if we will only take the time to go out and listen. Job knew something of this: "ask the animals, and they will teach you, or the birds in the sky, and they will tell you; or speak to the earth, and it will teach you, or let the fish in the sea inform you." (Job 12:7-8.)

Garden Prayer Stations

To get you started, here are some ways to take your small group out into a garden or park and worship God outdoors. You can find printable instructions and some further ideas at engageworship.org/GardenPrayerStations

Desert

You will need:

A spot with dry ground where nothing is growing, or a pile of dry earth or sand on the ground, or use a tray/sandpit.

A Bible, or printed copies of Matthew 4:4-11 and Psalm 42.

What to do:
Stand by your barren ground and read Matthew 4:4-11. Invite people to handle the dry earth and think about deserts. What is there? What is lacking?

Think of some words to describe the feelings of Jesus in the desert. What power did Jesus use to battle with the enemy?

Then invite people to think of times when they have found themselves in the wilderness, in a spiritual drought, where they lacked more than they had. What were their temptations at those times? How did they battle them? Think about how they can respond to temptations in the future, taking their lead from Jesus.

Then read Psalm 42 and make it your prayer in the desert.

Water

You will need:

A water feature in your garden, or put out a paddling pool, or other container, and fill with water.

Cut ovals or rectangles of cellophane or acetate plastic, in proportion to the size of your water.

Fine permanent markers.

Bible or print-out of scriptures: John 4:14, John 7:37-39, Revelation 21:6; 22:17.

What to do:
Read the scriptures listed above.

Reflect for a moment on Jesus' wonderful promise to give us the Water of Life. Think about why Jesus used this term to describe the Spirit; how is God like water?

Think of a word that describes this (for example: refreshing, life giving etc.), write it on a piece of cellophane and let it float on the surface of the water.

Spend a moment reflecting on God's goodness and receiving refreshment from him.

Fruit

You will need:

A tree or fairly substantial bush. It doesn't have to be a fruit tree.

A bag of cheap apples, permanent markers and string (if you don't like wasting food, you can cut the apples up, excluding the ink, and make a pie afterwards!).

What to do:

Read the following Scriptures: Matthew 7:15-19, John 15:4-5, Galatians 5:22-23.

Invite people to reflect on these questions:

What would it look like for you to bear the Fruit of the Spirit listed in Galatians 5?

Beyond this, what other kinds of fruit could a Christian bear?

Is there fruit that you feel that you ought to be bearing, but aren't?

Is there fruit that you long to bear, but haven't yet?

Bring all these thoughts before God and form them into a prayer. Sum up these thoughts and write them on apple, then hang it in the tree, presenting these prayers and longings to God.

Thorns

You will need:

This is an ideal station to choose for those of us with untidy gardens! Find the most weed- infested place in the area you're using, and centre this station there.

Provide a few gardening gloves.

What to do:

Read this passage, where Jesus explains the parable of the sower: Matthew 13:1-9, 22.

Invite people to spend a moment reflecting on the weeds you can see around you. What are they doing to the plants that were meant to grow there? What resources are they using up?

Consider the worries of your life. How are they stopping you from growing and bearing fruit? Are there specific worries that are particularly sapping you of life? How about the "deceitfulness of wealth" that Jesus speaks of? Allow God to speak into your hearts on these issues.

If you feel that there are worries that you need to hand over to God, do so. Then pull up a weed as a symbol of your new freedom to grow. Consider the space left in the earth once the weed has been pulled up. Pray that God would fill the space in your heart where the worry was, with spiritual growth and fruit.

> "You will find more labouring in the woods than you ever will among books. Woods and stones will teach you more than you can ever hear from any master."
> Bernard of Clairvaux, 12th century monk, quoted in Gary Thomas, *Sacred Pathways*, page 47.

We have compiled a whole book of ideas for engaging with God in his creation - see it at: engageworship.org/OutdoorBook

SIMPLE SUNDAY WORSHIP

We used to work for a church which put a lot of emphasis on sung worship with big bands. One year we went away on a church weekend, and we took a whole van full of PA, drums, keyboards, amps and projection screens. We put a lot of effort into setting up, rehearsing, and choosing the "big" songs which we felt would generate a response. But by the end of the weekend there was no escaping the feeling that the worship had somehow been empty; that we had been "going through the motions".

Then it hit us. We had not once stopped and prayed - committing the times to God, asking for his empowering, listening for his direction. We had relied on the technology, the popular songs and our musical capabilities more than the Spirit of God. So when we got back we determined to stop having a full band for the season of Lent. We would only use, at most, a single worship leader with perhaps a guitar or keyboard. We sang simple songs. We left space and silence. And in the times that we would have spent rehearsing, we instead gathered the worship team to pray, to re-focus on God, and to trust him again. (You can read a fuller version of this story in our book *How Would Jesus Lead Worship*, chapter 5).

Worship idols

It is important to note that the things we relied on were not bad in themselves. Music, technology and songs are gifts from God. Using them is not wrong. The mistake is to *rely* on these things, to put them on a pedestal as having power or status above God. The Bible has a name for things we treat in this way: it calls them "idols". There is a very real danger that we can begin to worship "worship": our perception of how worship ought to be done.

God himself set up the Old Testament worship laws, yet he is highly critical when Israel tries to use them as an end in themselves - as if he can be "bought" with a sacrificial offering, or a great song, or a wonderful prayer. The prophet Micah says:

> "What can we bring to the Lord?
> Should we bring him burnt offerings?
> Should we bow before God Most High
> with offerings of yearling calves?
> Should we offer him thousands of rams
> and ten thousand rivers of olive oil?
> Should we sacrifice our firstborn
> children to pay for our sins?
>
> No, O people, the Lord has told you
> what is good, and this is what he
> requires of you:
> to do what is right, to love mercy,
> and to walk humbly with your God."
> *Micah 6:6-8 (NLT).*

St Augustine spoke of sin as the problem of "dis-ordered loves" - that when we sin we take good things, good gifts of God, and love them in the place of God. In your church it might be that having a full rock band, new songs and charismatic worship leader has become a dis-ordered love. Can you worship God without them? Would it help you to have a season where you intentionally stripped these things back, in order to remember what the heart of worship is really about?

More than songs

It may be that, for your church, relying on songs and bands is actually not your temptation. In fact you may not have a worship band, and it might be a struggle to include even something as new as "Shine, Jesus, Shine" in your services. But that does not mean that you cannot fall into worship idolatry.

Think for a moment - what is it that you, or your church, rely on most in worship (apart from God)? Are you:

> - Obsessed with projection screens, videos and multimedia?
> - Determined to have exactly the right words, prayers and rituals?
> - Pre-occupied with making every aspect "seeker-sensitive" and impressive for guests?
> - Overwhelmed with including ever-more creative and artistic ideas?
> - Excessively devoted to using an extensive range of hymns and polished classical music?

Most of us have times when we find ourselves dependent on things in an unhealthy way. It is almost certainly a good thing; something you are passionate about and gifted with; something that God wants to use in you. Yet he does not want you to elevate this thing above him. And perhaps, for this reason, it is good to sometimes strip that thing away in your church worship for a while.

How and when?

It may be that you choose a season, such as Lent or Advent, or another period to "strip-back" your worship to more basic elements. Or it might be something that you do once a month, or a couple of times a term. A third way would be to take a short section of the service each week to do something intentionally "simple".

It is important that you frame what you're doing in positive terms. Avoid saying "we

are giving the band a break", or "we use the screen too much", or "we are fed up with the way worship has been led in the past..."! Instead, focus on the positive: you are going to have a time when you can engage with God more simply. You are going to explore other ways of worshipping, which you believe will deepen the congregation's faith experience.

What can you do?

Across this book we have provided a whole range of ideas of how you can choose simpler, more stripped-down worship. Some of these will not be relevant for your context, or they may be things that you already do regularly. The important thing is that you find the ways to worship that turn you away from substitutes for God.

So for example, if you know you over-rely on a projection screen, engage in some worship which involves reading direct from printed Bibles or hymn books. You could do away with written texts entirely, and use

very simple repeated prayers, songs and phrases. For visual stimulus you could use a physical artwork instead of a projected video, or you could light a candle, or encourage the congregation to look out of the window and be inspired by God's world.

On the other hand, if the issue in your church is an over-complicated liturgical structure, could you engage in a much simpler format for a season? Experiment with a Taizé-style service which involves short, repeated chants and brief scripture readings followed by long periods of silence. Or explore something like a Tenebrae service, which is based around readings and candles (see page 34). These are just suggestions - the important thing is that what you do (and don't do) should be appropriate for your context.

Returning to complexity

We hope that periods of simplifying worship will make a lasting impact. Congregations are likely to be blessed by stripped-down forms, reminded of the centrality of God, and encouraged to even take these forms out into their everyday lives of worship. You may continue some of the "simple" forms beyond the initial period.

However, there is something powerful about bringing complexity back in worship, even just for special occasions. In our church when the Lent period ended we re-instated the band for a huge Easter celebration service. The worship was enriched by bringing together the heart of the stripped-down time with the creativity and energy of the resurrection party. You might focus your energies on occasional special services, establishing a helpful rhythm of simplicity and celebration throughout your church's year.

> "Be still, and know that I am God."
> *Psalm 46:10.*

Some questions for reflection/discussion:

What might be your "worship idol" - something that you risk relying on more than God to make worship "happen"?

What would it look like to strip back your church's worship for a season, focussing on God more than the outward activities of music, technology, language, creativity...?

What fears do you have about simplifying your gathered worship? Share these with God, and ask him to speak to you about them.

THE LORD'S PRAYER

One of the key resources given to us by Jesus himself can be almost forgotten by modern church worship. We might preach a sermon on it, or look at it in a Bible study, but do we really engage with God through the Lord's Prayer on a regular basis?

The people of Israel had particular prayers that they said daily, by heart. It has been suggested that Jesus was developing this idea when he gave his disciples the "Our Father": giving us a prayer to repeat regularly so that we might be formed by its words into the likeness of Jesus. (See Scot McKnight, *The Jesus Creed*, chapter 2.)

Connecting with daily life

Shaping your gathered worship around the Lord's Prayer will help your congregation use it meaningfully in their everyday lives. You could invite people to take up the challenge from the 24/7 Prayer movement, to set a daily alarm and join thousands of others around the world, praying this at midday.

24-7prayer.com/lordsprayer

Singing the prayer

There are a number of settings to sing the whole prayer. Modern ones include Marcus Meier's "Our Father", and Matt Maher's "As it is in Heaven", more traditional versions can be found in hymn books and online. Find one that suits your congregation, or even write your own version. Teach it to your congregation so that everyone knows it by heart. You can then use it at any time without even necessarily needing to project or print the words.

Video version

The Church of England made an engaging video of the Lord's Prayer called Just Pray (which was famously banned from British cinemas). See it at:

youtu.be/vlUXh4mx4gl

It involves people in a whole variety of life situations, praying or singing the prayer. You could show this, and then invite the congregation to reflect silently, or discuss in groups. Questions could include:

- Is there a character in the video to whom you relate?

- Which line of the Lord's Prayer speaks to you most at the moment?

- How could you re-write that line in your own words, so it expresses what you want to say to God?

As an extension of this idea, you could take all of the re-written lines and combine them into a version of the Lord's Prayer which is unique to your church. You could use this alongside the traditional version, print it on cards for people to take home, or share via text or social media.

Use the prayer to structure a worship time

The idea is to simply read a line of the prayer together, and then for the leader to encourage the congregation in various actions of prayer and worship. The instructions are printed on the opposite page, and a free downloadable PowerPoint can be found here:

engageworship.org/LordsPrayer

If you are not sure whether people will immediately join in with "open prayers" from the congregation, you could prime a few people to be prepared to start things off. There is also a part where people turn to the person next to them - again, you may have to adapt this depending on how comfortable you think your congregation will be.

It then moves into two silent sections of prayer, and at the end we suggest you sing the final "doxology" part. We have written a simple setting in Bb - the music is printed below. The idea is that the music is "unfinished", ending on the F chord, which could then lead you into another song in Bb seamlessly. Alternatively, you could use another setting, or write your own.

Lord's Prayer Worship Structure

Our Father in heaven
hallowed be your name.
[Open prayers of praise.]

Your Kingdom come,
your will be done,
on earth as it is in heaven.
[Open prayer for situations that need God's reign to be evident.]

Give us today our daily bread,
[Share one need with the person next to you, and pray a short prayer for God's provision.]

and forgive us our sins,
as we forgive those who sin against us.
[Silent time of confession and forgiving others.]

And lead us
not into temptation
but deliver us from evil.
[Silence to receive God's Spirit - to lead us and sanctify us.]

[Music could begin to play here - in Bb if moving into the final sung setting suggested.]

[Sing:]
For the Kingdom, and the power,
and the glory, are yours *[repeat]*
forever, and ever, and ever,
Amen.

SILENCE

There is very little silence in our world. We are so used to the noise of cars, music, voices and general background clatter that silence can feel quite awkward and threatening when we first rediscover it. However, if we can lead a congregation sensitively into silence it is almost certain that they will find it refreshing.

People will probably find it helpful to know what they are supposed to be doing when everything else stops. One or two sentences can help people settle themselves into silence. Explain that you will take a moment's quiet:

- to listen for God's voice,
- to pray for the world,
- to reflect on a talk or a Scripture verse,
- to receive from the Holy Spirit,
- to just "be" in God's presence... and so on.

It can also be helpful to set a limit to how long the quiet period will be, for example say: "let's be still to listen for anything God might be saying, and then in three minutes we will move on with a song..."

Songs into silence

You can lead people into a time of silence with a song that sets up our need to be still. Some useful ones include:

- "Be Still And Know" (there are many settings of this text, including two by John L Bell and Graham Maule of the Iona Community).
- "Still (Hide Me Now)" by Reuben Morgan.
- "Calm Me Lord" by Margaret Rizza.

The beauty of your peace

The Christian denomination the Society of Friends (or "Quakers") traditionally include no singing in their worship, but sit in silence waiting for the "still, small voice" of God. One of their poets, John Greenleaf Whittier, wrote a long poem which, in part, critiqued hyped-up, loud and overly emotional worship. This was eventually set to music and has become a much-needed reminder of God's call for us to quieten down in his presence. The music and revised words are printed below.

You could sing this song reflectively as an introduction to a time of silence. Or you could read it as a poem, perhaps with the tune being played instrumentally. Another alternative is to use the Tim Hughes version, "Your Voice Has Stilled (Beauty of Your Peace)".

Words: John Greenleaf Whittier. © This version of the words by The Jubilate Group, www.jubilate.co.uk
USED BY PERMISSION. Line 2 of verse 5 adapted by Sam Hargreaves.
Tune: "Repton" by C. Hubert H. Parry (simplified chords by Sam Hargreaves), public domain.

Scripture and silence

Another way to introduce silence is to use a relevant Bible passage. Psalm 46 is ideal, as it moves from the noise of mountains falling, waters roaring, nations in uproar and weapons of war into God's command: "be still" (or some versions have "be silent"). You could simply read this, drawing out the dynamics with your voice. Or you could accompany the reading with sound effects, or with musicians improvising underneath - the sound can swell and grow more discordant, then die away to silence.

Poems into silence

In 1 Kings 19:1-18, God speaks not in the fire or wind but in "the sound of sheer silence". This story has inspired the following poem. Reading a poem like this is another way to introduce people to the idea of silent worship and reflection:

> God in the gaps
> That still small voice
> That sheer sound of silence
> Not in the expected dramatic happenings
> But in the unusual
> In the gaps
> In that thin moment after breathing out
> Before breathing back in
> In that whispery pause before the service begins
> And the shuffling lull as it comes to an end
> In the unexpected places
> The un-spiritual zones
> The surprising moments
> The disorganised moments
> The disruptive moments
> In the shadowed nooks
> In the dusty corners
> In the cluttered places
> The Monday mess
> The Tuesday chores
> The Wednesday work
> And the Thursday thankless tasks
> When everyone around is expecting something else God arrives
> In strange disguise
> In the gaps.

You could encourage the congregation to reflect in silence about the other "gaps", the silent moments in their lives, where they could give God the opportunity to speak. Thanks to Dave Hopwood for allowing us to use his poem, which was inspired by a talk by Paula Goodyear. See more of Dave's writing at: davehopwood.com

POSTURES

It is easy to find our minds wandering when invited to pray silently or reflect in church. Many of us are also natural "fidgets" who need to be moving or fiddling with something. Intentionally including and being aware of our physical body in worship and prayer reminds us that God is interested in our whole selves, and focuses both our posture and our minds on engaging with him.

Hand prayers

The following set of hand prayers is based on one by Andy Stinson, originally written for Ash Wednesday (the first day of Lent). The service was intended to be very simple, with lots of room to pray and included long periods of silence. He simply read out the words below (without the titles) pausing briefly at the end of each line and leaving a much longer pause at the end of each section.

Not only is this idea useful in a gathered worship service, but it can also offer a model that people could take out with them into their lives, their "quiet times" or their moments of prayer at work or on the bus.

The ideas could be easily adapted for use in all-age services, with sections added in or taken away to suit your situation. Consider other hand positions you adopt through the day and work out what they could help you pray about, or what is relevant to your community at the moment.

Introduce by saying something like:

To aid our focus whilst praying, I will invite you to make and hold physical positions with your hands. We do this to engage our bodies within our prayers, allowing our minds to focus more freely on what we are praying about.

Praying hands

First place your palms and fingers flat together, with your hands pointing upwards; in the position traditionally adopted to pray.
We come to be still before God.
Our hands together, stopping us undertaking physical work.
We take up the work of an intercessor, bringing our earthly concerns before our Heavenly Father.
"Answer me when I call, O God of my righteousness.
You set me at liberty when I was in trouble;
Have mercy on me and hear my prayer." (Psalm 4:1.)

Praising hands

Now lift up your hands, pointing your palms towards heaven. The book of psalms tells us that this is a way of honouring and blessing God. We surrender to him. We direct our praise to him.
What part of God's character do you want to praise him for?
What has God done in your life that you can be thankful for?

Fists

Separate your hands. Clench them together to form fists. Hold them as tightly as you can, so that your focus is on your fists.
We pray for those parts of the world afflicted by violence.
We remember those in violent relationships.
Where talking has been replaced by fighting.
Where peace has been replaced by aggression and unrest.

Wounded hands

Open both your fists. Hold your left hand so your palm faces towards you. Take the index finger on your right hand and push it hard into the centre of your left palm.
Jesus' hands were pierced as he was crucified.
He was wounded to restore our relationship with God.
He suffered to bring reconciliation and justice to the world.
We pray for situations and places where that reconciliation is needed, both in our own lives, our community, and the wider world.

Open hands

Open both of your hands. Hold them open in front of you with your palms facing upwards.
We recognise that all of humanity needs to receive good things.
God provides for each of us physically, emotionally and spiritually.
We ask God for the things we need, and the things needed by others.

Holding hands

Turn over your left hand, with your right hand gently take hold of your left as if holding someone else's hand. [Or you could invite people to actually hold each other's hands.]
Jesus embodied God's compassion.
He met with the sick and the dying. He promised comfort to those who mourn.
We pray for those who are sick, suffering or mourning.
We pray that they will know God's healing, comfort, compassion, and love.

Praying hands

We return our hands to the first position we held. Palms and fingers flat together, hands pointing upwards; the position traditionally adopted for prayer.
We remember God's promise to hear our prayers.
Praying to the Father, in the name of the Son by the power of the Holy Spirit. Amen.

Other postures

As well as hand prayers, other forms of physical posture can help us engage in worship. The Bible is full of different ways in which people move their bodies when approaching God: bowing (Ps. 95:6), looking up (Mark 6:41), lifting hands (1 Tim. 2:8), dancing (Ex. 15:20) and so on.

With any kind of worship like this, be sensitive to people with physical disabilities who may not be able to move in the same way as you can. Also be aware of people who are shy or lack confidence to engage in this kind of interaction. Introduce such activities by saying: "I am going to invite you to..." or "You may find it helpful to...". If you are concerned that people might not be able to join in, you can add "...or another gesture that is appropriate for you."

Here are some ideas, but you can also invent your own:

Kneeling

This is a sign of reverence, submission and humility. You could include kneeling when you are confessing sin to God, or praying for a particularly difficult situation. Additionally, if you are reflecting on God's power and kingly rule it might also be appropriate to invite people to kneel.

Facing different directions

When praying for your town or different parts of the world you can ask the whole congregation to face in particular directions. For example, you could face North when praying for your local schools that lie North of your building, or East when praying for China. Or you can face particular parts of your church building - pray for the children whilst facing the crèche, pray thanks for Christ's sacrifice whilst facing the communion table, offer prayers of praise looking at a stained glass window, and pray for tomorrow's work while facing the door.

Taking off shoes

In Eastern cultures taking off shoes is a sign of respect - see Exodus 3:5. In Western cultures it is often related to relaxation and feeling at home. You can draw out both of these meanings when inviting people to remove their shoes during worship.

Walking prayer

The church in 4th Century Jerusalem was not limited to one particular building, but moved around to different spots of the city depending on what aspect of Jesus' life they were remembering. This is called "stational" worship. (See Lester Ruth, *Walking Where Jesus Walked: Worship in Fourth-Century Jerusalem*, page 22.)

A series of "stations" for worship were also developed along the *Via Dolorosa*, the road that Christ is believed to have walked on his way to the cross. This idea was taken to other churches across the world, with small pictures representing each stage of the journey. These "Stations of the Cross" show a rich heritage of worship which involves walking, reflecting and interacting with creative rituals.

Labyrinths and prayer walks

You can follow in this tradition of walking worship, for example by setting up a prayer trail in your church garden, or a reflective labyrinth (see labyrinth.org.uk for ideas). All of these get people out of their seats and connecting with God in simple, evocative ways. Alternatively, take people outside of the church building on a prayer walk through your town. Encourage them to listen for God's still, small voice as they walk, and pray silently for people and situations they see as they pass homes, shops, play areas and businesses. Gather back together and discuss what you were praying for.

PRAYER STATIONS

Following on from walking prayer, it is quite simple to set up prayer stations around your church for people to interact with. We like this because there is a sense of unity and diversity - each person engages at the level appropriate for them, but you are all worshipping together in the same room.

Setting up your own

The subject of the stations can vary depending on context - for example they could be:

- Reflecting on a teaching theme, Bible passage or a season of the church year.
- Personal stations where the individual contemplates their own life before God.
- Praying for other people and parts of the world.
- A mix of the above, and more.

There is no one "right" way to set up a prayer station, but we have found the following tips to be helpful:

Have a clear aim

What is the main point of each station? Do you want people to: confess sin, thank God, reflect on the past, pray for an issue, ask questions, hand something over to God... or something else? Avoid each station being either vague or over-full.

Have something visual

A prop, a painting, a video loop, a newspaper, a cracked mirror, a bowl of fruit... whatever relates to the theme and engages people visually.

Make it biblical

Print out a verse or a passage which roots your reflection in God's word.

Encourage an action or ritual

Stations work less well when they only ask the user to "think about" such and such. Instead, involve an activity: write your prayer in sand, pick up the heavy bag, destroy your sin in a paper shredder, put a post-it note on the mirror... whatever is relevant to your aim.

Clear instructions

Make sure the instructions are pithy and make sense (get someone else to read them and check if they understand them). Print them big enough so everyone can read them.

Make sure stations are accessible

Consider who will be using them, and how to make each station as accessible as possible. It can be better to have small tables rather than placing things on the floor, and to put some chairs near each station. If there are people with particular needs such as limited eyesight or mobility, consider how they can access the stations. Make sure there is enough of everything - four small stations for a congregation of 100 people means you could have 25 people crowding around each station, so spread things out and have enough props and instruction sheets.

Word of God stations

We put the following stations together on the theme of "Word of God". You could adapt this for your own use, or just see it as an example to inspire your own kinds of stations. Instruction posters and further stations can be found here:

engageworship.org/WordPrayerStations

Honey

You will need:
Instruction posters.
Bottle of squirty honey.
Disposable tea spoons.
Paper and pens.

Instruction Sheet:
Psalm 119:103 - "How sweet are your words to my taste, sweeter than honey to my mouth!"

Taste a spoonful of honey as you reflect on this Scripture. Think back to a time when this has been your experience, when a word from God has provided sweetness or soothing in your life. Thank God for this.

Write a couple of sentences on a piece of paper to sum this experience up, and leave it here as a testimony for others to read.

Silver and Gold

You will need:
Instruction posters.
Bowl filled with £1 coins.

Instruction Sheet:
Psalm 119:72 - "The law from your mouth is more precious to me than thousands of pieces of silver and gold."

Grab some coins from the bowl. Feel the weight of the coins in your hand. How does it feel to hold money? Does it make you feel excited? Happy? Anxious?

What are your priorities in life? Would you be prepared to make less money if God asked you? Do you give more time to making and worrying about money, or to be with God? Spend some time reflecting on this Scripture, then realign your life with it.

Light

You will need:
Vase with fairy lights, or candles.
Bibles.

Instruction Sheet:
Psalm 119:105 - "Your word is a lamp to my feet and a light to my path".

Think about areas in your life where the path is dark and unclear. Spend some time in prayer asking God for guidance. Open a Bible and read.

Alternatively, ask someone else to pray for you at this station; ask them to listen to God for you and share any words from him.

Prayer for Bible translation

You will need:
Instruction posters.
Bibles in different languages.
Prayer points sheets.
Tub of play-dough and paper towels.

Instruction Sheet:
Psalm 119:130 – "Break open your words, let the light shine out, let ordinary people see the meaning".

The full Bible is available in 554 different languages, giving 5,054 million people access to Scripture in the language they understand best. There are over 2,267 active projects worldwide, yet work needs to be done in a further 1,800 languages (see wycliffe.org.uk).

Pray for God's Word to be available to every language group. Use play-dough to create a symbol of your prayer.

CANDLES

In many churches candles are lit every week. In other contexts they might only come out for Advent or a candlelit carol service. There is a rich tradition of worship which engages with the symbolism of a simple candle flame. Jesus is the Light of the World (John 8:12); he calls us to shine that light in the world (Matt. 5:14); and however dark it gets, the darkness cannot overcome Christ's light (John 1:5).

Tenebrae

A Tenebrae (Latin for "darkness" or "shadows") service can be a very simple, symbolic use of candles and darkness. They are commonly held on Good Friday, as a sombre way of journeying with Jesus through the passion story. The church should be lit minimally at the beginning, except for one candle per Bible reading and a central candle representing the light of Jesus.

At the end of each reading, one of the candles is extinguished. This goes on until the final reading where Jesus dies, and the Christ candle is blown out. Traditionally there is not a neat, positive "resolution" to the service - we are left, with the first disciples, in a symbolic darkness that anticipates Easter Sunday. It is up to you whether you also include songs, a sermon, times of led prayer and so on. It seems to us that the readings, the candles and a time of silence may be sufficient, creating space for God to speak at a deep level.

SIMPLE SUNG WORSHIP

We have included many worship ideas in this book which do not involve music. We hope they will be useful to you. But another area which is neglected in the contemporary church is the art of simple singing. Whether it is Israel celebrating with tambourines and dancing after being saved from Egypt, Jesus and the disciples at the Last Supper, Freedom Songs in Apartheid South Africa, the repeated chants of the Taizé community or the choruses of the early Charismatic Renewal - Christian worship has a rich heritage of people turning to God with little more than a few words set to a simple tune.

told "you cannot sing". In church, our music often relies on technology, accompaniment and strong leadership in order to function. For this reason, what happens in church often stays in church.

This is not the case in many non-Western contexts, and nor has it been for most of church history. Singing can be a communal event which everyone participates in, and the songs are then carried out into everyday life, work and leisure. The aim is not necessarily musical perfection, but the unity-in-diversity which comes from joining with all kinds of other voices. This is a powerful and sacred thing. As John Bell puts it:

Professionalisation

One issue we face in today's world is that music has become "professionalised". Certain people are elevated onto stages as singers. Songs are technologically enhanced and designed for performance rather than community. A good proportion of people are

"Something extremely rare happens whenever a congregation sings to its Maker. For not only are there ten or fifty or five hundred individual voices giving their unique gift as they open their mouths and sing: there is also the unique blending of high and low voices, sharp and flat, sophisticated and rough-tongued, male and female, old and young. The chances are that never again will every one of these people be in exactly the same place singing these particular hymns and songs... So if we can sense it, every time a congregation sings, it is offering an absolutely one-time-only gift to its maker. It is important that every song sung is offered to God with that sense of uniqueness. God is worth it."

John L. Bell, *The Singing Thing*, page 80-81.

It can be assumed that, in order to sing well, groups must have either a band, an organ or pre-recorded backing tracks. While these can be useful, it has been our experience that one way to encourage singing is to actually have less accompaniment. The more a congregation can hear themselves sing, the more they are likely to sing out.

Four tips for simple sung worship

In order to facilitate this, we want to suggest a few pointers:

1) Choose simple singable songs

"Performance" songs with complicated melodies and wide vocal ranges that require skilful instrumental accompaniment have their place, but these are not the same as congregational songs. Look for songs with a fairly narrow range which will be inclusive of most voices (e.g: A below middle C, to C# or D an octave above middle C). Melodies should be catchy and full of repetition. Syncopation is not necessarily a problem if it follows natural speech rhythms, but avoid needlessly tricky tunes.

2) Lead confidently

Teach a new tune line-by-line, encouraging the congregation to sing after you. Use a microphone to be heard if necessary, but avoid making your vocal performance the centre of attention. Instead, see yourself as a choir leader, enabling the whole group to sing. Feel free to step back from the mic once they get going. Use words of encouragement - "you sound great!" - catch people's eyes and smile.

3) Use instruments wisely

Sometimes voices alone can be the most effective solution (see idea on following pages about a cappella singing). Other times you might want to include just a guitar, a piano, or something more unorthodox such as a ukulele, an accordion or a junk percussion group. If you do include larger numbers of instruments, think about how they are adding-to and supporting the singing, not competing against it.

4) Think about the worship space

If people are spread out and facing the front, they are unlikely to have a sense of a group singing together. If possible, move the chairs or the people so that they are facing each other. Acoustically, some spaces are more reverberant and encourage singing, whilst others kill sound as it leaves your mouth. If you get to choose your venue you might want to find a place that enhances vocal music.

A question of repetition

Songs and hymns with a lot of verses are great for unpacking themes, expressing important truths and telling stories. We should not lose these. But there is also something profound about a simple, biblical phrase which we repeat until its meaning shifts from our heads to our hearts - what the Bible calls "meditation" (e.g. Ps. 77:12).

When we combine this with appropriate music, the impact of the repetition deepens. Brian Wren writes of Taizé songs:

> "Though simple, they are neither empty nor trivial... repetition of the words can enable us to let go of our left-brain constraints and become more open to wonder, mystery and transcendence."
> Brian Wren, *Praying Twice*, page 202.

Words set to music sit in a different part of our brain, so that even those suffering from poor memory or dementia can often remember songs they learned in childhood. Without even realising it, words that we sing lodge deep in our hearts and shape our thinking about God, the world, and ourselves. John Witvliet says: "What more soul-shaping force can we imagine than the songs we sing?... Music has the uncanny ability to burrow its way into our spiritual bones" ("The Cumulative Power of Transformation in Public Worship" in Alexis D Abernethy (ed.) Worship that Changes Lives, page 47).

This means that we should think carefully about what it is we are repeating. Do the words of your simple songs make sense? Are they rooted in scripture, and/or church history, and true to your experience? How are they shaping the people singing them?

Framing

Also consider how you "frame" a simple lyric. Take the ancient prayer Kyrie Eleison, "Lord have mercy", for example. How would this be received, if sung within these different "frames":

- Sung after reading the story of the Pharisee and the Tax Collector (Lk. 18:9-14).
- Sung with a bright melody, in a major key.
- Sung with bluesy, discordant, minor harmony.
- Sung with images of a natural disaster on a screen.
- Sung after a period of silence, where people consider their own mistakes from the past week.
- Sung with the lights out in a low whisper, remembering those who worship in secret?

Ultimately, keep in mind to whom you are singing. Simple worship should draw us back to focus on the author of song: God.

> "Sing to the Lord a new song, his praise in the assembly of his faithful people."
> *Psalm 149:1.*

Some questions for reflection/discussion:

What do you think is the difference between speaking and singing worship to God? Why do you think the Church historically has sung so much?

Do you have an experience of singing very simple songs, with little or no accompaniment? What was it like?

Read the quote from John Bell on page 35. He describes a wonderful perspective; how can you encourage this kind of attitude in your context?

HALLELUJAH

One of the most basic expressions of Christian worship is "hallelujah" (sometimes written "alleluia") - from the Hebrew, meaning "praise the Lord". It is an exhortation to ourselves and others - God is worthy of praise. He is to be revered and glorified.

Singing Hallelujah

We once heard a very simple version led by Brian McLaren. He encouraged the congregation to sing the word hallelujah on the first note of the scale ("doe"), then on the second ("ray"), all the way up to the fifth ("so"). We then went back down the scale and ending on the first note again. This was completely unaccompanied. Quite quickly the group took their attention off the music and lyrics, and focussed their attention on singing praise to God.

Ha - le - lu - jah, ha - le - lu - jah, ha - le - lu - jah, ha - le - lu - jah,

ha - le - lu - jah, ha - le - lu - jah, ha - le - lu - jah, ha - le - lu - jah, ha - le - lu - jah.

Other simple settings

- Ben Cantelon's "Hallelujah (Be high and lifted up)".

- The chorus of Brian Doerksen's "Your Love is Amazing".

- the chorus to the Leonard Cohen song (although some people struggle with using this in worship as they cannot disassociate it from its original, secular setting).

These can work a cappella or with minimal accompaniment, such as a guitar or piano.

Our friend Chloe Axford wrote a poem about the word Hallelujah. You could use this to introduce a time where you sing the word and encourage people to bring their praise to God however they're feeling.

Hallelujah - what does it mean?
Not a translation, but a transliteration,
an anglicised version of two Hebrew words -
Hallelu - to praise joyously, to boast in God, and
Jah - God, Yahweh, Jehovah.
It's not so much a statement as an instruction -
praise God, you peoples,
praise God, all creation,
praise God, O my soul.

Spoken all over the world, for thousands of years,
in countless dialects and contexts.
Sung with majesty in Handel's chorus,
shouted with joy in spontaneous praise.
And oftentimes declared as a choice,
through tears,
in the face of doubt,
in the midst of pain.
Sometimes it's a cold and it's a broken hallelujah.

Each utterance is the same, and yet totally unique.
What Hallelujah do you bring today?
Thankful and exuberant?
Tired and weary?
Uncertain and frail?
Because every Hallelujah is welcome here today,
welcomed by us, welcomed by God.
So shout it, sing it, whisper it or just think it,
join with the angels and creation and peoples throughout history and time:
"stand before the Lord of Song
with nothing on your tongue but Hallelujah".

SIMPLE SONGS

Doxologies

A doxology is a statement of praise to God - we find one in Romans 11:33-36. A well-known doxology is set to the hymn tune best known as "All People that on Earth do Dwell". Once learned, this can be sung confidently without instruments.

Praise God from whom all bles - sings flow.
Praise him all crea - tures here be - low.
Praise him a - bove you heav'n - ly host,
praise Fa - ther, Son and Ho - ly Ghost.

Public Domain

Choruses

The charismatic worship "chorus" came from evangelistic beach missions, where they did not have hymn books to hand and so just sang the choruses of well-known hymns. Think of choruses you know which could work like simple doxologies and be sung without texts: Fanny Crosby's "Praise The Lord" from "To God Be The Glory", Matt Redman's "Bless The Lord O My Soul" from "10,000 Reasons", Rich Mullins' "Awesome God", and so on.

Space for interaction

Another reason to use simpler songs is that they can allow space for congregational interaction. A fast chorus or a densely packed hymn do not encourage adaptation in the middle of the service, but a minimal, slow song can be tweaked "on the fly". This might be the role of the lead singer - repeating a line but changing a word or two to suit what God is doing in the moment. Or you could invite the congregation to shout out suggestions.

This is something we often do with Joel Payne's song "He's My Saviour". Not only does this great tune express the truth that "Christ has died, Christ is risen, Christ will come again", but it also allows the space for the congregation to suggest other attributes of Jesus. They might call out "He's my healer", or "How I love him", or "My salvation" and so on. Sometimes it might take the leader to make the suggestion fit, but we have found that this song always encourages heartfelt contributions from the congregation.

resoundworship.org/song/hes_my_saviour

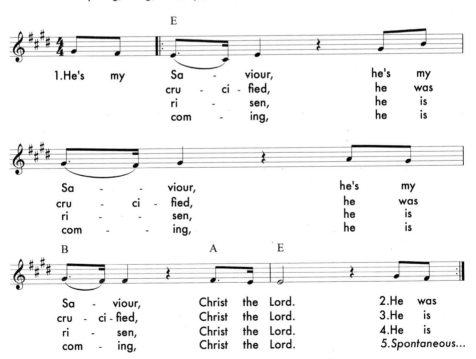

© Joel Payne/RESOUNDworship.org Admin by The Jubilate Group, www.jubilate.co.uk USED BY PERMISSION

SINGING PRAYER

Singing in the contemporary church is often linked to praise, thanks and intimate adoration. We sometimes forget that we can also connect our songs with our intercessory prayers for other people. In fact, doing so can help avoid the trap of sung worship becoming individualistic.

Refrains

You can use a short, repeated refrain to respond to situations in prayer. You might say "think of a problem you have seen on the news recently", or "bring to mind one person who needs God's loving care". Then encourage people to sing a line or chorus over the situation, singing it as a prayer of blessing, healing or God's intervention. Song suggestions include:

- The Taizé chant "O Lord Hear My Prayer".
- John L Bell and Graham Maule's "With God All Things Are Possible".
- The chorus of Noel Richards and Gerald Coates' "Great is the Darkness (Come, Lord Jesus)".

Below is a very simple refrain Sam wrote for this purpose. You can add-lib other lines as appropriate, e.g. "Send your power/Spirit/mercy..."

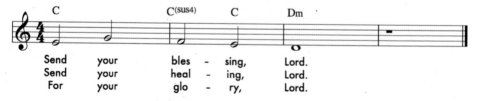

© Sam Hargreaves. Admin by The Jubilate Group, www.jubilate.co.uk USED BY PERMISSION

We have also done this with hymns and Christmas carols. For example, a simple setting of a couple of lines from "O Come, O Come Emmanuel" can be sung out over a situation, as a reminder that Jesus is not just "God with us" at Christmas but at all times and with all people, by his Holy Spirit and through his church. Find music for this idea here:

engageworship.org/PrayingCarols

R O U N D S

You might only associate rounds with children's songs. Although they may have that kind of simplicity, a good round is also quite a sophisticated piece of musical composition, as multiple lines and rhythms weave together in harmony. The unity-in-diversity of a round is a great illustration of the body of Christ, each line and each person being different, and yet so vital.

Introducing rounds

Teaching a round can be a great way to encourage a *cappella* singing. We have found that it is helpful to have a strong leader, probably on a microphone, for each part. It is also key to teach the parts clearly, so that everyone is confident of their line. Once they get the hang of it, the congregation begins to realise that it is important that they sing - their voice counts.

resoundworship.org/song/jesus_lead_us_to_the_father

© Sam Hargreaves/RESOUNDworship.org Admin by The Jubilate Group, www.jubilate.co.uk USED BY PERMISSION

Other suggestions for rounds:
- "Great is He Who's the King of Kings", author unknown.
- "Gloria" by Jaques Bertier, Taizé Community (taize.fr/en).
- "You're King" by Geraldine Latty and Carey Luce.
- "Wonderful Counsellor" by Andy Irons (RESOUNDworship.org).

Below is another great round by our friends Geraldine and Carey Luce. You can get more of Geraldine and Carey's fantastic music for community-choir singing from www.lucemusic.london

resoundworship.org/song/spirit_of_god

CALL-AND-RESPONSE

The invention of the printing press, and later the overhead projection screen, changed the way we sing. Previously, songs were mostly kept in the memory rather than in written form. Songs like these are typically shorter, more memorable, and can evolve organically as they are used in different contexts. Although many of us have lost this skill, it is still a valued part of many cultures today.

Turn off the screen

There are great benefits to books and screens, but sometimes we might want to experiment with other ways of singing. Why not turn off your screen or put your books away, and encourage the congregation to do some more listening? You could sing very simple songs which require no printed texts, such as the ones suggested on the previous pages.

Alternatively, if you want to use longer songs, there are other methods for communicating lyrics. "Lining out" is used in gospel music, and involves a leader singing ahead of the congregation in the gaps, so that the rest of the church knows what to sing next. The idea can also be heard in the more traditional role of a "cantor". Both of these methods take practice and skill, but they can free you up to sing longer songs without printed texts.

A simpler version of this process is the call-and-response song. Written into this kind of song is a role for a leader to sing a line, which the congregation repeats. Printed on the next page is a song by Sam which uses this technique. If you teach the congregation the chorus first, the rest of the song can be learned immediately as you go through.

Give thanks to the Lord, (give thanks to the Lord), he's been good to us,
Give thanks to the Lord, (give thanks to the Lord), he's been good to us,
Give thanks to the Lord, (give thanks to the Lord), he's so good to us,

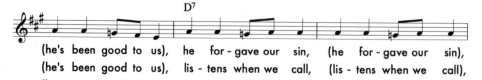

(he's been good to us), he for-gave our sin, (he for-gave our sin),
(he's been good to us), lis-tens when we call, (lis-tens when we call),
(he's so good to us), sat-is-fies our needs, (sat-is-fies our needs),

so we sing to him, (so we sing to him), died so we can live,
faith-ful when we fall, (faith-ful when we fall), mer-cy from your throne,
dis-ci-plines and feeds, (dis-ci-plines and feeds), he's our ev-'ry thing,

(died so we can live), Praise is what we give, (praise is what we give).
(mer-cy from your throne), hope in Christ a-lone, (hope in Christ a-lone).
(he's our ev-'ry thing) wor-ship Christ the king! (wor-ship Christ the king!)

Great is the Lord and most wor-thy of praise, great is the Lord most high,

Great is the Lord and most wor-thy of praise, great is the Lord most high.

Other suggestions for call-and-response songs:
- "I Will Worship" by David Ruis.
- "Because We Believe" by Jamie Harvill and Nancy Gordon.
- "Jesus You Are Lord" by Rick Founds.
- "Let Your Spirit Rise" by Judy Gresham (RESOUNDworship.org).

SPONTANEITY

Many churches would like their worship to be more spontaneous, but they struggle to know where to begin. Simpler worship can create space for this, allowing gaps where God can speak and you can be led into fresh avenues of encounter. One of the things you might try in this context is to make up a spontaneous song - responding to the moment by singing out a phrase that you feel is on your heart.

Be prepared

At this point, it is important to state what might sound like a contradiction regarding spontaneity: it requires practice. Yes, you need to prepare for the unprepared! We are not saying that you fake it - claiming to have improvised a song when in fact you were up all night writing it. Instead, in order to improvise well, you need to get used to doing it. Just like a jazz musician practices improvisation, so we can prepare for spontaneity by experimenting with it in our homes and in music rehearsals, making us ready to try it in front of other people.

Preparing musically

Experiment by singing a name of God, a line from a psalm or a worship phrase over some simple chords. If you are just starting with this, we would suggest beginning with the first chord in the key (e.g. in the key of C you would play a C chord), and the fourth chord (count four away from C, to an F). Repeat the C - F progression slowly and steadily.

Now sing your phrase with notes that feel like they fit with those chords. Keep the rhythm fairly straightforward. Is there a particular word which is important in the phrase? You can emphasise this by making that note longer or higher than the rest of the phrase, or by placing it on a strong beat such as beat one or three. If you are doing this in a group, take it in turns to share a phrase, and have everyone else join in. You will start to notice that some melodies can be picked up easier than others.

As you progress in your improvisation, you can begin to add other musical ideas. You could add chords five or six (G and A minor in the key of C), or substitute the F chord for a Csus4, or an F with a C bass note. You can think about the dynamics (volume) and the feel (beat, texture). What sort of music does the text suggest: quiet and peaceful; strong and powerful; light and joyful, ominous and lamenting...? If you have more than one instrument playing, encourage them to join in at appropriate moments, adding rhythms, counter-melodies, drone notes and other textures. Remember - in a rehearsal situation it is fine to "play", to experiment and make mistakes. This is how you will become more confident to step out within a real service context.

Preparing spiritually

When you improvise in a sung worship setting you are using your physical abilities as a musician, and you are bringing those together with a second aspect - your ability to discern God's voice. It is unlikely that you will suddenly be transformed into a virtuoso pianist or a professional singer - God gives gifts, and then he wants us to work on these aspects and improve them. But remarkable things can happen when we bring whatever musical skill we have and combine it with a heart that is listening for God's still, small voice.

For this reason, as well as preparing musically we need to prepare spiritually. Ask God to help you listen for his voice in your everyday life. You will probably find it helpful to experiment with this in a prayer partnership or small group. Ask God specific questions: "What is your will for this event?" "Show me your heart for this person." "How does this scripture apply to my life?" Listen for impressions, Bible passages, pictures or words. Very few people seem to hear an audible voice, but when we quiet ourselves we can sense God's prompting.

We should always test what we think we hear against God's character as revealed in the Bible, and also with other discerning Christians. We can then begin to walk and live in the light of what we think God has spoken. As we do this, we start to learn how to hear and obey God in a dynamic way. It is this kind of listening that we can bring to our times of leading worship. In our preparations and when in the midst of a congregational gathering we can be asking God "what should we sing, Lord?", "what is on your heart for this group?", "how can we pray for this situation?" This can then begin to spill over into your musical expression, singing out or playing your instrument in line with the way God is speaking to you.

SIMPLE CONTEMPLATIVE
W O R S H I P

Being present

How often do you find yourself truly *present* in the moment? Are you able to focus on what is happening right now, not what happened yesterday or what might happen tomorrow?

We live in an unusual time in history, where there are more attention-seeking devices around us than ever before. In trying to navigate the digitally powered 21st century, we have the capability to be never truly present. If we are bored or unhappy, there are always apps, websites or cute cat videos to take our mind off things.

This inability to be fully present has been called "hyper attention" - a way of being which "has a low threshold for boredom, alternates flexibly between different information streams, and prefers a high level of stimulation." (N. Katherine Hayles, *How We Think: Digital Media and Contemporary Technogenesis*, page

12, quoted by Shaun Lambert in *The Baptist Times*, 30/09/15.)

In worship services many of us are aware of this phenomenon. Church leaders are frantically trying to keep up with their members' seemingly ever-lowering attention spans. If we have catchier songs, snappier notices, smoother PowerPoint presentations, lights, smoke and the vicar entering on a zip-wire - then surely people will be more present?!

A need for contemplation

Outside of church, it is often the same, disjointed story. We might rush from meeting to meeting, eat lunch by our desks, take phone calls during family meals and flick through an unending list of channels on our TVs in the evening. And all through the day (and night, if we forget to turn them off), there are continuous "pings" from various digital devices, keeping us updated about news stories or letting us know that someone "liked" our selfie. The phenomenon of FOMO (fear of missing out) is dragging our attention away from the present - from our family members, friends, immediate tasks and even God.

We are everywhere, except in the present.

In some ways contemplation could simply be summed up in the word "presence", the ability to be in the moment. In the modern, secular version of contemplation - mindfulness - this means being present to yourself, your own emotions and inner being. It could mean being present in the moment with another person. In Christian tradition, we are invited to contemplate God, to be present to him in the moment.

Attention and Intention

Anthony the Great was one of the group of monastics in the 3rd century AD who became known as "the Desert Fathers" and whose contemplative practices are influential in the Church to this day. In an anecdote attributed to him, he was asked "What must one do in order to please God?" He responded:

> "Pay attention to what I tell you: whoever you may be, always have God before your eyes; whatever you do, do it according to the testimony of the holy Scriptures; in whatever place you live, do not easily leave it. Keep these three precepts and you will be saved."
>
> Benedicta Ward (translator), *The Sayings of the Desert Fathers*, page 2.

This desert father does not call on seekers to leave their community or their occupation to join the ranks of the hermits, but rather, he calls them to change the attitude with which they live their lives. To "always have God before your eyes" and to "not easily leave" where you are, might be filed under the heading *attention*. Are you attentive to God, his presence in and purposes for the world around you? Are you attentive to what is going on around you, being watchful and alert towards family members, friends and strangers you encounter during your day? Or do you "easily leave" - geographically or virtually - the places you find yourself in?

To do what you do "according to the testimony of the holy Scriptures" may be referred to as the *intention* of what you are doing. Do you know why you do what

you do? Why do you go to work every morning? Is it to earn enough money to live a good life? Or does it have a deeper meaning; has God sent you to be the best accountant, for example, that you can be? To do your work in a godly manner, "according to the testimony of the holy Scripture", as a loving, truthful, compassionate accountant, or whatever your calling might be?

The same questions can be asked of your leisure time: Do you know why you do what you do? What is the intention behind your evening activities? Whether you are in the pub, attending a church small group or staying in watching TV; the important question is not what you do, but how and why. As Thomas Keating puts it: "Far better to be present to your duty if you are a bartender than to be present in church and thinking about being in a bar." (Thomas Keating "The Practice of Attention/Intention", in Gustave Reininger (ed.), *Centering Prayer in Daily Life and Ministry*, page 17.)

Contemplative tools

Contemplative worship, with its emphasis on presence and the dual values of attention and intention, is helpful to the worshipper both in and outside of the church. We can learn to use various contemplative exercises within gathered worship, but we can also pick them up when scattered again. They can provide us with a focus, whether we find ourselves on a stressful commute to work, stuck on an uncomfortable chair feeding a baby, or bored in a waiting room. Contemplation offers us tools that we can use to draw near to God in our everyday lives.

Learning to be present to God, in church and in everyday life, does not need to be complicated. When Jesus asked his followers to contemplate something, he did not need projection software or a powerful sound system. He was present in the physical moment, encouraging his friends to "look at the birds of the air" and "see how the lilies of the field grow" (Matt. 6:26, 28) as a meditation on God's care and provision. Or in Matthew 18:2, "He called a little child to him, and placed the child among them..." and encouraged his listeners to consider how they could be more like this child.

What everyday things can you "consider" when you come together to worship? If you were to be fully present in the physical moment of gathering to worship, what might God reveal of himself and his plans for you? What intentions of your heart come to the surface in those moments?

The rest of this chapter will give you further practical and time-tested contemplative tools which can provide some structure if you want to have a go. None of these tools are set in stone or holy in themselves, and there is nothing stopping you from adapting them for your life or church context.

> "Cause me to understand the way of your precepts, that I may meditate on your wonderful deeds."
> *Psalm 119:27.*

Some questions for reflection/discussion:

How "present" would you say you are, living in the moment rather than focussed on the past or future? What distracts you?

What are your experiences of contemplation, meditation or reflection? Have you found these easy or hard, live-giving or a burden?

Are there places where aspects of contemplation might fit in your small group, Sunday gatherings or other worship times?

CENTRING PRAYER

"Centring Prayer" is a way of praying that aims to focus our contemplation on scriptural truth. The aim is not so much to have a conversation with God but more to simply enjoy his presence.

Anchor word

One way to engage in this is to take a name of God from the Bible and hold it before you - Father, Prince of Peace, Love, and so on. The idea is not to speak it out loud like a mantra, but to hold it, and repeat it in your mind as an anchor. When your mind wanders into your own concerns or worries, the idea is to recognise this concern but gently pull yourself back to your anchor.

Let words be few

You might feel uncomfortable using so few words in a prayer. If so, it's worth remembering Jesus' parable of the Pharisee and the tax collector in Luke 18. Here Jesus criticises the Pharisee's long, self indulgent prayer but lifts up the tax collector as an example for us, with his simple words "God, have mercy on me, a sinner" (Luke 18:13). One of the oldest Christian prayers recorded is the Jesus Prayer, based on the tax-collector's prayer: "Lord Jesus Christ, have mercy on me a sinner", repeated in silent meditation. In church worship, this prayer has been used since the earliest days, especially in its Greek form, *Kyrie Eleison*.

Within gathered worship

Is there a way that an element of centering prayer like this could be introduced into your gathered worship? Could a simple modern chorus (for example the chorus to the song All Who Are Thirsty - "Come Lord Jesus, come"), or a Taizé chant, or a simple setting of a prayer, offer you an opportunity to lead the congregation in focusing on God?

Alternatively, could you project a name of God onto the screen, and encourage people to turn it over in their minds and enjoy God's presence? Or as a response to a sermon, could you invite people to reflect silently on a name of God which summarises who they need God to be for them at that moment - Great Physician, Friend of Sinners, The Truth...?

It might be difficult at first - in our age of quick-fix solutions we may be disappointed that the first few times we engage in a contemplative practice it does not give us the same immediate spiritual "high" as our favourite worship song. However, like a healthy diet, the result of simple, reflective focusing on God will be to grow attention towards him. And the fruit of learning to be present to God will be the ability to be present to other people and the tasks God sets before us.

In our everyday lives

This tool of centring prayer is helpful for a Christian's everyday life as well. Often we find ourselves in periods of our lives where the demands are so high, that taking time out regularly for long quiet times seems like an impossibility. Finding moments to still ourselves and reconnect with God may require some ingenuity.

How about using your commute for a time of centring prayer? Whether it's a five minute walk or an hour's train ride, could you get into the habit of choosing an anchor word or phrase each day, and forsake podcasts or personal worries for that time in order to centre yourself on God?

You may have other times in the day to use, for example, if you have babies who require holding while asleep, or if you are in a job which has a lot of waiting around. Or it might be that you decide to take five minutes in the middle of the day to lock yourself in a toilet cubicle and still yourself. The hope is that you might then be more fully present - attentive - to your God-given work and relationships.

> "To be totally present to children if you have them, to the elderly if you have them... to the job of the present moment that needs a responsible fulfilment - this is what might be called how to act from the centre, how to do contemplative service, how to put order into ordinary life by being present to the occupation of the present moment."
>
> Thomas Keating "The Practice of Attention/Intention", in Gustave Reininger (ed.), *Centering Prayer in Daily Life and Ministry*, page 16.

LECTIO DIVINA

Lectio Divina (which means Godly Reading) is a particular way of reading the Bible and praying that stems from at least the 12th century. It is a simple practice, which enables us to slow down, refuse to run through a tick-list of engagement with God, and puts us in a place where we can hear God speak. There are four stages:

1) Lectio (reading)

Read a Bible passage in a calm and reflective way. You can do this yourself, reading out of your own Bible. There is, however, something special about doing this in a group, and hearing the Word read aloud. The passage should be read several times, and it is helpful on the second or third repetition to invite people to listen out for a particular word or phrase that jumps out to them - a particular word from God.

2) Meditatio (ruminating)

The second stage is contemplating or chewing on the text that you felt was highlighted. Repeat the phrase in your mind, and allow God to speak to you through those words.

3) Oratio (responding)

Oratio (which simply means "speech" in Latin) is the moment for "speaking" back to God, our response or prayer. What kind of conversation springs from what God has spoken - praise, thanks, questions, intercession for others, confession for sin, commitment to live differently...?

4) Contemplatio (resting)

This is a silent stage, where we can be still and enjoy God's love and presence. Put words to one side and just be with God.

This activity could take anything between five minutes (if you are using only a few verses) to 30-45 minutes for a longer passage and a slower rhythm. Over the page is a script of how you might lead a Lectio Divina. Feel free to adapt or rewrite it in your own words.

Getting over concerns

If you have never engaged in *Lectio Divina*, you may feel sceptical. Perhaps you lead a group of people who believe that they cannot hear God speak? We have shared those fears in the past, but have been delighted to see that this simple structure helps people. In the humble expectation to hear God through his Word, life-changing messages have been received and the gentle, encouraging presence of God has been encountered.

The structure explained above is not a magical formula, nor is it copyrighted, so we would encourage you to be creative and consider what would work best for your context.

In different groups and settings

We find that play-dough is an excellent accompaniment to *Lectio Divina*: it is a great tool for anyone who struggles to focus and be still, and it can help us form our thoughts. During the reading section you may simply knead it in your hands, but gradually towards the meditation stage the dough might have become something which represents the word you've had illuminated. You can then literally look at your word from all angles in your meditation. It is easy in the response stage to re-form your shape into a symbol of your prayer. This is good for adults and children, and in the same way you could use paint or encourage drawing.

For more literate groups, you could actively encourage writing, perhaps in mind-map style, or maybe ask the group to create a poem in the response stage to share later.

This activity works well with children too, but you need to make sure that the passage is short and all the thought processes are allowed to happen out loud (for example, by sharing in groups after each section).

If you think your group will feel unsafe when thrown into a quiet reflection without knowing where they are going, make sure you explain beforehand that the reflection will have four stages, and perhaps put the names of the stages on a projection screen or a handout to give people a road map. Another helpful idea is to have a candle for each stage which you light as you enter the next stage – this would also give you a nice visual focus, for those who feel concerned about keeping their eyes closed for longer periods.

Lectio Divina Example Script

We are going to listen to God now, and have a chance to respond to him too. We will do this using the exercise called *Lectio Divina* which is simply a structure for reading the Bible and praying, with four steps: Read, Ruminate, Respond and Rest. If you struggle keeping thoughts just in your mind, feel free to doodle or write. But let's start by being still before God.
[Pause for group to get comfortable/get pen and paper.]

Father God, we come before you. Thank you that your Word is living and active. Please, speak to us through your Word right now, open our ears to hear you, open our hearts to receive you. We come through Christ. Amen.

It might help you to close your eyes, and I'm going to read a passage of Scripture, from *[insert Bible reference]*, just relax and listen.
[Read passage once or twice depending on available time and length of the passage.]

I'm going to read the passage again, and this time I want you to be observant to any word of phrase that jumps out at you. Perhaps it's as if a particular word becomes illuminated in your heart as I read it. Feel free to note anything down, doodle or draw as you listen.
[Read again – pause.]

I invite you now to meditate on what you have heard. Take the word or phrase that stood out to you and turn it over in your mind and in your heart. Repeat it to yourself, ruminate on it, look at it from all different angles. What is this word from God for you?
[Longer pause.]

I'd like to invite you now to respond to this word of God, to turn your word into a prayer. What is your word or phrase calling you to? What might the action or application be to what God has spoken? What will your response be? Talk to God about that.
[Pause.]

The final stage of our reflection is to simply be. Put aside your own agenda, the chattering of your mind, and be still before God. Bask in his presence and allow deep to call to deep.
[Pause.] Amen.

EXAMEN

Examen comes from the Spiritual Exercises of Ignatius of Loyola, a 16th century Jesuit. The aims of these are well summed up in his often-repeated prayer:

> "Lord, grant that I may see thee more clearly, love thee more dearly, follow thee more nearly."

Five steps

The idea is to take some time out to examine your day in a prayerful way. St. Ignatius' *Examen* has the following five steps:

1. Become aware of God's presence.
2. Review the day with gratitude.
3. Pay attention to your emotions.
4. Choose one feature of the day and pray from it.
5. Look prayerfully towards tomorrow.

Using the steps of the *Examen* is a helpful way to end a day, but they can also be used at other times. There are natural pivot points in time, such as the end of a working week going into the weekend, at the end of a term going into a holiday, or in the change between seasons, where an *Examen* can be a useful tool for reflecting backwards and looking forwards in a prayerful way.

To give you an idea of how you might lead an *Examen*, over the page is the script for an end-of-day prayer time, which we encourage you to adapt into your own words

Adding creativity

There are ways to add variety to an *Examen*. You could print a timeline with the questions about different periods, for people to work through individually. On the opposite end of the spectrum, you could pause after each stage of reflection and discuss the questions together in groups. For children and young people, it might help to make the activity as visual as possible; a printout of an empty clock face and a variety of stickers (saying "thank you", emoticons expressing emotions, and so on) could be helpful.

Example Examen Script

We're going to engage in a kind of *Examen* prayer. It is an ancient and simple way of bringing your life before God. It's going to have five steps, which are all fairly straight-forward, and I'll guide you into each step. Some of us struggle to keep thoughts and prayers just in our minds, and it helps to have pen and paper, or something to fiddle with. During this activity you can write, doodle, draw, scribble - no one is going to look at it unless you decide to show it to someone. If you're writing, it might help you to make a timeline of the day at this point.

So, the first step is to still yourself. For me it helps to close my eyes and try to put other distractions to one side. In Matthew 28:20, Jesus says: "I'll be with you ..., day after day after day, right up to the end of the age." God is present with us right now; acknowledge his presence in your heart, and rest in it. You are safe, at rest, nothing to prove, and God is here.

The second step is to think through the last day - and to remember it with thankfulness. Try to remember the hours that have led up this moment, and each time to find something that you are grateful for to God, pray a little "thank you!" in your heart, or add a little squiggle on your time line. Take some time over this, allowing God to remind you of all the good things in your life. *[Pause.]*

Thirdly, we are going to think about the emotions that have been present in the last day. If you're writing, you might want to reflect on each stage of the day and add a drawing of a face reflecting how you felt at that moment. *[Pause.]* What are the over-riding emotions in your heart? Bring your emotions before God, in all honesty. Allow him to shine his light on them, showing his perspective. *[Pause.]*

Fourthly, now choose just one thing that stands out in your day - either something that worries you, puzzles you or evokes some other kind of emotion. Shape it into some sort of prayer, either in words or pictures. What does this memory draw you into: praise, confession, prayer for others...? Bring this thing before God. *[Pause.]*

Finally, look towards the coming day. What are your dreams and hopes? Do you have concerns that you want to mention to God? Spend a moment reflecting on or scribbling this. *[Pause.]*

[End prayer:] Father God, who was there in our past and who promises to be with us in the days to come, we bring all these prayers to you. Thank you for the things you have reminded us of, thank you for hearing our cries for help. Go with us now, into the rest of this evening and onwards. In Jesus' name. Amen.

GUIDED MEDITATION

To meditate on something means to think about it carefully and purposefully. Often, thoughts about God and our relationship with him might come to us in church or small group, but we struggle finding the time and space to really reflect on them. In these instances, a guided meditation can be very helpful, as the person leading it can help us focus our minds, and open us up to hear from God.

Potential topics

You could prepare a guided meditation about almost anything which deserves thinking about. It helps if the leader encourages the listeners to enter into the meditation using their imaginations and all of their senses.

Engaging imaginations

For example, you may want to lead your group in a meditation about how they can be a blessing to people in their work place. It is then helpful to guide your listeners in reflecting on their various senses, for example:

"Imagine that you are in your workplace. Look around you, what can you see? What sounds can you hear? Are there any distinctive fragrances in this room? Imagine that you're sitting or standing where you spend most of your time - what can you feel? Do you sit on a chair - what does it feel like? Do you touch any objects - do they feel smooth, rough, warm or cold?..." and so on.

Once your group has firmly located themselves in the place they imagine, they can start making other observations, such as "Can you see anyone you can bless?" or "How can you make this place better or more beautiful?".

Bible meditation

We like using guided meditations for reflecting on Scripture. It is easy to rush through a passage of the Bible and to miss what God wants to speak to us about. Slowing down and thinking about the setting, the scenery and the characters in a story can help us make space for God's voice. Over the page is a guided meditation on the passage about Elijah on Mount Horeb. You can use it in your context and let it inspire you to write your own meditations.

1 Kings 19:8-13 Guided Meditation

[Do add a suitable, down-to-earth introduction for your own setting, giving the option of closing eyes and relaxing. Explain that this guided meditation is a simple way of using our imagination in Bible reading. Remember to pause after the questions and to read slowly.]

I want you to imagine that you are in a different country, and the climate is hot and dry. You look around you and see that you're in a desert. What can you see around you? What does the ground look like? There are mountains on the horizon - what do they look like? What colours can you see?

Take a deep breath through your nose, what can you imagine the desert air smelling like? What are the fragrances coming from? Breathe in through your mouth, what does the desert air taste like? Lift your eyes up to the sky - what does it look like? What do the sun and the wind feel like in your face?

Some way off, you see a man walking steadily towards you. You stay still and watch him, and as he comes closer his features become clearer. The man looks very tired, worn down even. You see a matted beard and a simple, dusty cloak. This is the prophet Elijah.

As he walks steadily closer to you, make an image in your mind of this man. He has been walking for forty days and nights - imagine his walk. Is he using a stick or not? Is he walking without problem, or is he displaying pain anywhere? What do his feet look like after walking such a distance? Imagine what his hands look like.

As Elijah's face comes into focus, you sense fear and anxiety in his expression. Imagine his eyes, his skin, his mouth.

You follow the prophet at a distance when he walks past you. Imagine the sound that your feet make as you walk across the dry ground. Feel the heat on your face as you keep walking.

You reach a mountain, and you sense that there is something special about this mountain. There is a presence as you start following Elijah up a path on the side of the hill; you sense holiness and power. This is Horeb, or Sinai, the mountain of God.

The prophet seems to be looking for something, craning his neck, searching behind bushes. He finally stops and you see that he has found the opening of a cave. What does the opening look like? Imagine the darkness as you peer inside.

Elijah enters the cave and curls up in a corner. You see his face in a small strip of light from the opening. What emotions can you see in his face now? Imagine his eyes and his mouth. Is he sitting or lying down?

Suddenly you hear a voice that startles you. "What are you doing here, Elijah"? it says. What does the voice sound like? Spend a moment thinking about the question; you realise that it's the voice of God - why would he ask this question?

You see that Elijah is not startled at all by the voice, but that the emotion on his face intensifies and he straightens his back to answer. Imagine Elijah in the half-dark of the cave answering God. He says:

"I have been very zealous for the Lord God Almighty.
The Israelites have rejected your covenant, torn down your altars,
and put your prophets to death by the sword.
I am the only one left, and now they're trying to kill me too."

What does Elijah's face look like as he pours out his heart before God? What emotions is he expressing? What did his voice sound like?

You hear the voice of God responding:

"Go out and stand on the mountain in the presence of the Lord for the Lord is about to pass by."

What does hearing this make you feel? What's your emotional response to these words? What emotions does Elijah's face show?

Just as the sound of God's voice dissipates, you hear the wind outside the cave picking up. The strength of wind increases, until you start seeing large displaced rocks tumbling past the opening of the cave, and bushes and trees pulled out by the roots. Imagine the noise of the wind and clattering of pebbles and rocks. How does all this make you feel? Imagine Elijah's face.

The Lord was not in the wind.

As the wind dies down, you notice to your dismay that the ground seems to be moving. You realise that you are caught in an earthquake, and you grab what you can to keep yourself upright. More rocks break off from the mountain, tumbling down the steep slopes with a great crash. Imagine the confusion and the sense of urgency. Imagine Elijah's face.

The Lord was not in the earthquake.

As the earthquake slows down and the mountain gradually comes to a stand still, you realise how tense your muscles are and you begin to relax. Then a quiet sound, growing all the time, comes to your attention. It's the unmistakable crackling noise of a fire, and soon you sense the sharp smell of smoke in your nostrils. The fire spreads quickly and grows to a roar outside the cave, and great clouds of smoke drift over you. Imagine what this feels like in your mouth and nose. You can't see Elijah through the smoke; imagine what his breaths might sound like.

The Lord was not in the fire.

As quickly as the fire had begun, it suddenly dies down and the smoke gradually drifts out of the cave to be replaced by fresh air. Take a deep breath.

Finally, there is complete silence in the cave. It is so quiet that you can hear your own heartbeat. You listen for any noise, and, almost so quiet that it's not there at all, you can hear a gentle whisper.

The whisper was like nothing you had heard before, but you sense the holiness and the presence of God. What emotions are you experiencing?

You realise that Elijah must be recognising the whisper as the presence of God, because you watch him pull his cloak over his head and move towards the opening of the cave.

You watch the prophet clamber out of the cave. What expression is on his face? Desperation? Expectation? Fear? Exhaustion? Does he move fast or slowly?

He makes it just outside of the mouth of the cave, and stands there, completely still.

Sense the stillness and the holiness of this moment.

Finally, you hear the voice of God again:

"What are you doing here, Elijah?"

Now, imagine God asking the same question of you today. He knows your name; he calls you by name: "What are you doing here?"

What will you answer?

SABBATH

Someone sent me a link a couple of years ago to an article by a journalist in a Swedish financial newspaper. The journalist was writing about this new "life method" that he had discovered; a new way of living which, the headline stated, could protect you from burn-out and stress. Intrigued, I read the article and found that his revolutionary way of living involved working for six days and then completely resting on the seventh day. Genius! Why has no one thought of this before? (Quick, trademark the term 6:1...)

I joke, of course. As Christians we recognise this pattern as an ancient and biblical one. We know that God stopped (in Hebrew, *sabat*) creating on the 7th day, and rested instead. We know that he asks us to do the same. In the midst of a list of very serious commandments, God speaks these words to Moses on the holy mountain:

> "Six days you shall labour, but on the seventh day you shall rest; even during the ploughing season and harvest you must rest." *Exodus 34:21*.

For most of us modern urban (or at least suburban) people, ideas about agriculture probably pass us by. "God commands his people to have Sabbath" we hear, and then "something, something about farming." However, if you listen extra carefully to this verse, you might hear the pregnant pause in the semi-colon.

Farming and illogical rest

I [Sara] grew up on a farm, where my father's mood was entirely dependent on the weather. He was impossible to please - one day he was grumpy because the weather was too cold to sow, but (it seemed to me like) the next day was wrong because it was too hot for the newly planted seeds. It needed to rain at the exact right moments, except, of course, on the days when the sun had to shine. If one of those perfect days fell on a Sunday he was torn, I'm sure, as he was very specific about the Sabbath (I was not allowed to play any games that might look like work to an outsider). But in the end, he'd head out to the fields, probably in the hope that God is reliably gracious, whereas the weather is reliably unreliable.

That's why I hear this in that pregnant pause in verse 21:

"Fine, we'll work six days and then rest the seventh. Sounds good actually, we're up for that... Except of course when we're too busy to rest, I mean when it's good weather for ploughing it's good weather for ploughing, the next day might be bad weather. And the harvest doesn't wait for anyone, if the grain is ripe, it's ripe. The next day it may rain and the harvest will be ruined. That's logical right, God?"

But God replies: "Even during the ploughing season and harvest you must rest."

There is no logic in resting during ploughing time and harvest - if I rest today when the weather is good, there are no guarantees that the weather will be good tomorrow when I pick up my plough again. Now, most of us don't have the responsibilities of agriculture on our shoulders, but we do other work. "Harvest time" for a salesperson might be closing a deal - would you take a day off in the midst of that? Many of us work towards deadlines - would you close your laptop lid for a whole day when the deadline is looming?

A different day

When Moses repeats God's commands to the gathering of Israelites in chapter 35, he says: "...for six days, work is to be done, but the seventh day shall be your holy day, a day of Sabbath rest to the Lord" (verse 2).

Moses calls the day of rest "holy". The seventh day will be different from the other days, it will be counter-cultural, it will be "in the style of God." To actually rest on the seventh day says something profound about who God is, and who we are in relation to him - whether we are farmers, salespeople, parents, pupils or retired. Resting when work needs to be done is to proclaim that actually I'm not God, my sustenance actually depends on God, not me. I'm saying that my survival and success are not down to me, they are down to God. He is God and I am not.

God is asking us to stop. To be still. Know that he is God.

A truer Sabbath

Working all hours is to be confused about who is God in our lives. To stop is an act of faith. Laying down my plough is a sacramental act; it points to a truth deeper than "humans need rest." We read in the New Testament that Christ has fulfilled the law, that there is nothing we can do to add to his work (Hebrew 10). In his death on the cross, Christ ushered in a truer Sabbath rest. We do not need to labour, as in the Old Covenant, with animal sacrifices and complex legal systems, but can rest in the salvation Christ has won for us.

And yet, we labour. We do this in our personal lives, where we never switch off, sacrificing family time, quiet time and rest time to meet our deadlines, because somewhere deep inside we still believe that it depends on us. We also do this in church.

What are we really saying with our packed-out service structures and frantic Church calendars? Do we somewhere deep inside still believe that it depends on us? That we somehow need a bigger screen, a better drummer, a more impressive altarpiece, a smoke machine or a younger crowd in order to worship God? When all along "...we have been made holy through the sacrifice of the body of Jesus Christ once for all" (Hebrews 10:10).

Saying no

I know of one or two churches who keep saying "yes" to everything. Every ministry someone suggests, every visiting speaker coming their way, every new resource, every new song... Sabbath tells us that sometimes we have to say "no" to things. Not for the sake of grumpily shaking our heads at anything new coming our way, but for the sake of being more present to God.

You can see this spelled out in Matthew 6, where Jesus encourages us to reject things which will be a distraction from being present to God. We are to give to the needy, but without telling other people about it (v2-4). We are to go into a room alone to pray (v 6). If we refrain from food sometimes, only God should know about it (v 16-18). We should be aware of not storing up treasures earth rather than in heaven, and make sure that money is not taking the place of God (v 19-24). Finally, Jesus lets us know we don't need to worry about food or clothes but to "seek first [God's] kingdom and his righteousness,